I FINALLY FOUND THAT BOOK I'VE BEEN WANTING TO GET YOU...

HOW NICE!

"DARWIN AND THE BEAGLE"

BIRDS HAVE SOME PECULIAR ATTRIBUTES...

WHEN BIRDS FALL ASLEEP ON TREE BRANCHES, THEIR CLAWS AUTOMATICALLY TIGHTEN TO KEEP THEM FROM FALLING OFF...

WHICH CAN BE VERY HARD ON THE BRANCHES...

OR SOMEONE'S NOSE!

Madam Fullcharge

I'M READY!

SO IT'S "SHOW AND TELL" TIME AGAIN, IS IT? WELL, DO I EVER HAVE A SURPRISE FOR YOU TODAY!

I HAVE A LITTLE FILM TO SHOW YOU THAT'S GONNA KNOCK YOUR EYES OUT!

NO, MA'AM... THAT'S ONLY AN EXPRESSION..

ALL RIGHT, IF I CAN HAVE A COUPLE OF YOU STRONG TYPES LIFT THIS PROJECTOR INTO PLACE, WE CAN GET THIS SHOW ON THE ROAD!

NO, LET'S PUT IT ON THAT TABLE BACK THERE... HOW ABOUT YOU FOUR WEIRDOS MOVING THAT TABLE?

AND I'LL NEED A COUPLE MORE TO PUT THIS SCREEN UP... LET'S GO!! ON THE DOUBLE, THERE!

STRETCH THAT CORD ACROSS THE BACK, AND PLUG IT INTO THAT SOCKET IN THE CORNER...

OKAY, SOMEONE RUN DOWN TO THE CUSTODIAN THEN, AND GET AN EXTENSION! YOU THERE, GET GOING!!

NOW, WHAT ABOUT THOSE WINDOW SHADES? LET'S HAVE ALL OF YOU WHO SIT ALONG THE SIDE THERE PULL DOWN THOSE STUPID SHADES..

AND I'LL NEED SOMEONE ON THE LIGHT SWITCH... ONE VOLUNTEER... YOU THERE, HONEY, GET THE SWITCH!

IS THAT THE BELL ALREADY?

OKAY, WE'LL TAKE IT TOMORROW FROM HERE.. EVERYONE BE IN PLACE BY NINE! THANK YOU, AND GOOD MORNING!

SCHULZ

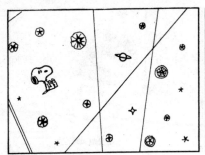

ALL RIGHT! CUT IT OUT!!

YOU CAN STOP DOING THAT ANY TIME!

I SAID CUT IT OUT!!

I KNOW WHAT YOU'RE UP TO!

SHE WANTS TO BE THE TALLEST ONE IN OUR FAMILY...

EVERY TIME SHE WALKS BY, SHE PUSHES DOWN ON MY HEAD TO KEEP ME FROM GROWING!

Why dogs are superior to cats.

They just are, and that's all there is to it!

SHORT AND TO THE POINT!

I CAN TELL ALL ABOUT YOU BY FEELING THE BUMPS ON YOUR HEAD...

COME BACK HERE! DON'T YOU WANT ME TO READ YOUR HEAD?

NO WAY!

FORGET IT...

THAT CAN HURT WHEN YOU TURN THE PAGES!

OKAY, I'LL MOVE...

HE SAID I WAS VIOLATING HIS BODY SPACE!

THERE'S A STRANGE LIGHT IN THE SKY...

THAT MEANS THE WORLD IS COMING TO AN END...

WHENEVER A STRANGE LIGHT APPEARS IN THE SKY, IT MEANS YOU HAVE TO GET READY FOR THE WORLD TO COME TO AN END...

WE'RE READY

Winter had come again all too soon, and it was time for Joe Jacket to bring in his polar cows.

As he rode out from the barn, the first flakes of snow began to fall.

He looked up at the slate-gray sky and shivered.

The blizzard started quickly. A howling wind pounded the snow across the bleak prairie.

Joe Jacket hunched forward in the saddle, and urged his mount forward through the flying snow and screaming wind.

TELL MY PUBLISHERS NOT TO EXPECT A MANUSCRIPT UNTIL SPRING!

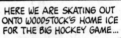HERE WE ARE SKATING OUT ONTO WOODSTOCK'S HOME ICE FOR THE BIG HOCKEY GAME...

AND HERE COME THE OFFICIALS...

THE REFEREE

THE LINESMEN

THE GOAL JUDGES AND THE PENALTY TIMEKEEPER

THE OFFICIAL SCORER AND THE GAME TIMEKEEPER!

WHICH BRINGS UP A SLIGHT PROBLEM...

WHERE DO WE PUT THE ORGAN FOR THE NATIONAL ANTHEM?

SCHULZ

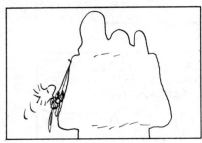

IF HE TRIES TO INSTALL A CABLE CAR AND A SUMMIT RESTAURANT, I'M LEAVING!

They had named their Great Dane "Good Authority."

One day, she asked her husband if he had seen her new belt.

"Belt?" he said. "Oh, I'm sorry. I thought it was a dog collar. I have it on Good Authority."

Shortly thereafter, their marriage began to go downhill.

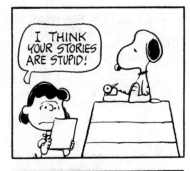

I THINK YOUR STORIES ARE STUPID!

IF THEY'RE EVER PRINTED IN A BOOK, I REFUSE TO WASTE MY MONEY ON IT...

HOWEVER, IF YOU GET SOME FREE AUTHOR'S COPIES, I'LL BE GLAD TO TAKE ONE!

BONK!

WHY CAN'T KIDS JUST DO THINGS ON THEIR OWN?

WHY DOES EVERYTHING HAVE TO BE ORGANIZED? WHY DO WE HAVE TO HAVE TROPHIES? WHO CARES WHO WINS?

IT'S NOT WISE TO LIE IN BED AT NIGHT ASKING YOURSELF QUESTIONS THAT YOU CAN'T ANSWER...

SCHULZ

WHAT WOULD HAPPEN IF I SNEAKED OUT INTO MY BACK YARD AND MADE A SNOWMAN WITHOUT ADULT SUPERVISION?

I'LL DO IT!

PSST, SNOOPY! WANNA HELP ME MAKE A SNOWMAN?

AT TWO O'CLOCK IN THE MORNING?

CALL ME WHEN THE SNOW IS WARMER!

SCHULZ

ZIP!

RAH

THINGS LIKE THAT
COULD RUIN SPECTATOR
SPORTS...

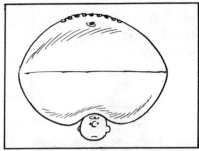

DO YOU LIKE JOKES AND RIDDLES?

I GUESS SO... WHY?

I HAVE A RIDDLE FOR YOU, CHARLIE BROWN... WHAT ARE THE THREE THINGS IN LIFE THAT ARE CERTAIN?

DEATH AND TAXES!!

THAT'S ONLY TWO...

YOU'RE RIGHT... HMM... I KNOW WHAT THE THIRD ONE IS, BUT I JUST CAN'T SEEM TO THINK... DON'T TELL ME...

RATS! I SEEM TO HAVE A MENTAL BLOCK OR SOMETHING...

IT'S SO AGGRAVATING WHEN YOU'RE TRYING TO THINK OF SOMETHING, AND YOU...

NOW, I REMEMBER!

WHAM!

IT WAS SO OBVIOUS, CHARLIE BROWN!

She wanted to live in Canada.

He wanted to live in Mexico. Thus, they parted.

Years later, when asked the reason, she replied simply,

"I just didn't like his latitude!"

IT'S ALWAYS THE SAME...

HELLO AND GOODBY!

THIS IS WHAT HAPPENS ON HALLOWEEN NIGHT, MARCIE...

THE GREAT PUMPKIN RISES OUT OF THE PUMPKIN PATCH, AND FLIES THROUGH THE AIR AND BRINGS TOYS TO ALL THE CHILDREN IN THE WORLD!

I'VE HEARD ABOUT YOU

SIR, DO YOU BELIEVE IN THE GREAT PUMPKIN?

THE GREAT WHAT?

LINUS SAYS THERE'S A GREAT PUMPKIN WHO BRINGS US TOYS ON HALLOWEEN NIGHT

THE WORLD IS FILLED WITH WEIRD PEOPLE, MARCIE...

I'M FINDING THAT OUT, SIR!

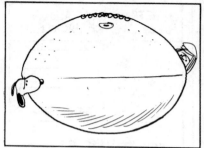

"Our love will last forever," he said.

"Oh, yes, yes, yes!" she cried.

"Forever being a relative term, however," he said.

She hit him with a ski pole.

YOU CAN'T SLEEP ON A COLD NOSE!

GOOD MORNING, CHUCK...BOY, WAS THAT EVER A LONG NIGHT!

WHAT I NEED IS A ROUSING BREAKFAST...

HOW ABOUT A STACK OF HOT CAKES WITH TWO FRIED EGGS, SOME SAUSAGE, ORANGE JUICE AND A SLICE OF MELON?

WHICH KIND OF COLD CEREAL WOULD YOU LIKE?

YES, MA'AM...I'D LIKE TO TRANSFER TEMPORARILY TO YOUR SCHOOL...

MY DAD IS OUT OF TOWN, YOU SEE, AND I'M STAYING IN CHUCK'S GUEST COTTAGE SO I'LL BE GOING TO THIS SCHOOL FOR AWHILE IF YOU'LL HAVE ME...OKAY?

I'M NO GREAT SCHOLAR, YOU UNDERSTAND, BUT I'M ALWAYS IN THERE TRYING...

IF IT'S "TRUE OR FALSE" OR "MULTIPLE CHOICE," I'LL BE IN THERE WITH THE BEST OF 'EM!

HELLO, CHUCK? SAY, HOW WOULD YOU LIKE TO HAVE A HOUSE GUEST?

ME! MY DAD'S GONNA BE OUT OF TOWN FOR AWHILE, AND I CAN'T STAY HERE ALONE...

YOU COULD STAY AT **MY** HOUSE, SIR!

NO, I HAVE ABSOLUTELY NO PLACE TO STAY! GEE, I APPRECIATE THIS, CHUCK..

WE HAVE LOTS OF ROOM AT MY HOUSE, SIR!

boot!

I'LL BE OVER AS SOON AS I PACK...THANKS, CHUCK!

YOU KIND OF LIKE CHUCK, DON'T YOU, SIR?

SCHULZ

WHERE WILL YOU SLEEP WHILE YOU'RE AT CHUCK'S HOUSE, SIR?

IN THE GUEST ROOM, OF COURSE!

I'M SURE THEY HAVE A GUEST ROOM...CHUCK'S DAD IS A BARBER...BARBERS ARE RICH..

ONCE YOUR SCISSORS AND YOUR COMB ARE PAID FOR, THE REST IS ALL PROFIT!

I DON'T THINK YOU KNOW MUCH ABOUT BARBERS, SIR...

STOP CALLING ME "SIR"!

SCHULZ

I DON'T KNOW WHAT'S WRONG WITH MY PASS RECEIVER...HE KEEPS COMPLAINING ABOUT HEADACHES...

GOOD MORNING, MISS... I'M SELLING A NEW ITEM FOR KITTENS, AND I..

FOR WHAT?

FOR KITTENS...THIS IS A NEW TOY I HAVE DEVELOPED...A KITTEN CAN ENTERTAIN HIMSELF FOR HOURS WITH THIS TOY'...

THE TOY IS SIMPLICITY ITSELF... I HAVE TAKEN SEVERAL PIECES OF SCRAP PAPER AND I HAVE CRUMPLED THEM UP...

A KITTEN WILL PLAY FOR HOURS WITH A PIECE OF CRUMPLED PAPER! HE'LL BAT IT, AND HE'LL JUMP AT IT...

AND IF YOU HANG IT FROM A STRING, HE'LL HIT IT AND BOX WITH IT AND EVERYTHING!

IT'S REALLY FUN TO WATCH A KITTEN BOUNCE AROUND...

WOULD YOU LIKE TO BUY ONE? THEY'RE ONLY FIVE CENTS APIECE..

WHY SHOULD I BUY ONE? WHY CAN'T I JUST CRUMPLE A PIECE OF PAPER MYSELF?

ALL ALONG I'VE BEEN AFRAID THERE WAS SOMETHING WRONG WITH THIS IDEA...

His wife had always hated his work.

"You'll never make any money growing toadstools," she complained.

"On the contrary," he declared. "My toadstool business is mushrooming!"

She creamed him with the electric toaster.

"Do you love me?" she asked.
"Of course," he said.

"Do you really love me?" she asked.
"Of course," he said.

"Do you really really love me?" she asked.
"No," he said.

"Do you love me?" she asked.
"Of course," he said.
So she asked no more.

SSSSSS!!

BLEAH!

SOMEBODY'S ALWAYS STIRRING UP THE ENEMY!

HA! YOU DIDN'T THINK I COULD GET MENTIONED, BUT I DID!

I DON'T KNOW WHAT YOU'RE TALKING ABOUT..

THE SCHOOL PLAY! THE PROGRAM WHERE EVERYONE GETS MENTIONED!

SEE? THEY HAVE THE NAMES OF ALL THE KIDS WHO WERE IN THE PLAY, AND THEY HAVE THE NAMES OF ALL THE ADULTS WHO HELPED WITH SCENERY AND FOOD AND THINGS...

WHERE DO YOU COME IN?

WHERE DO I COME IN? JUST READ THAT LAST LINE... YOU'LL SEE...

"SPACE DOES NOT PERMIT THE LISTING OF ALL THOSE WONDERFUL PEOPLE WHO GAVE THEIR TIME AND EFFORT WHEN NEEDED"

BY GOLLY, DON'T TELL ME I'M NOT IMPORTANT ENOUGH TO GET MENTIONED!

I'M COMPLETELY CONVINCED!

Theme: Our School

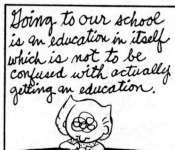

Going to our school is an education in itself which is not to be confused with actually getting an education.

I DON'T NEED THAT KIND OF TROUBLE!

MISS OTHMAR...

IF I WERE TO BRING A TV DINNER TO SCHOOL TOMORROW, WOULD I BE ALLOWED TO USE ONE OF THE OVENS IN THE CAFETERIA TO HEAT IT UP?

I SEE

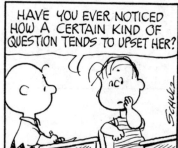

HAVE YOU EVER NOTICED HOW A CERTAIN KIND OF QUESTION TENDS TO UPSET HER?

Gentlemen,

Well, another day has gone by and you still haven't come to pick up my novel for publication.

Just for that, I am going to offer it to another publisher.

Nyahh! Nyahh! Nyahh!

RATS!

IT'S HOPELESS!

IF I'M GOING TO WORK AT NIGHT, I'M GOING TO HAVE TO HAVE AN INDOOR STUDIO...

YOU CAN'T WRITE BY FIREFLY!!

Gentlemen, I have just completed my new novel.

It is so good, I am not even going to send it to you.

Why don't you just come and get it?

Gentlemen,

Yesterday, I waited all day for you to come and get my novel and to publish it and make me rich and famous.

You did not show up.

Were you not feeling well?

Their Love Was Not in the Cards

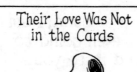

"You've always ignored me," she said. "And now you say you want to marry me."

"Every night you play cards."

"I'm really afraid," she said, "that you love cards more than you love me."

"If you could say something nice to me just once, perhaps I'd marry you."

" ◇ ♣ ♡ ♠ "

"You blew it!" she said, and walked out of his life forever.

STRIKE THREE!

DON'T WORRY, SNOOPY, YOU'LL GET TO BAT AT LEAST TWO MORE TIMES...

BY THE WAY, TEETH MARKS ARE NOT GOOD FOR YOUR BAT...

ALL RIGHT, SNOOPY, IT'S THE NINTH INNING...

THIS WILL BE YOUR LAST TIME AT BAT THIS SEASON...IF YOU'RE GOING TO TIE BABE RUTH'S HOME-RUN RECORD, YOU'VE GOT TO DO IT NOW!

CHARLIE BROWN'S ON SECOND... A HOME RUN WILL TIE THE RECORD AND WIN THE GAME! IT'S HERO TIME, SNOOPY!!

I JUST WANT TO BE A CREDIT TO MY BREED!

BABE RUTH HIT SEVEN HUNDRED AND FOURTEEN HOME RUNS...

THAT HAS TO BE ONE OF THE MOST FANTASTIC RECORDS IN THE HISTORY OF SPORTS...

BUT SNOOPY HAS HIT SEVEN HUNDRED AND THIRTEEN HOME RUNS! HE ONLY NEEDS ONE MORE TO TIE THE RECORD...

JUST A LITTLE OL' COUNTRY BOY DOIN' HIS JOB!

STRIKE THREE!

IF YOU'RE GOING TO BREAK BABE RUTH'S HOME-RUN RECORD, YOU'RE GOING TO HAVE TO DO BETTER THAN THAT...

AS YOU SEEM TO KNOW...

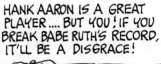

SEVEN HUNDRED AND ELEVEN...

SEVEN HUNDRED AND TWELVE... SEVEN HUNDRED AND THIRTEEN! I CAN'T BELIEVE IT! ONLY ONE MORE TO GO...

CHARLIE BROWN, DID YOU KNOW THAT ONE OF OUR PLAYERS CAN TIE BABE RUTH'S RECORD OF CAREER HOME RUNS THIS YEAR? DOES ANYONE KNOW THAT?

YES, I, FOR ONE, AM QUITE AWARE OF IT!

SNOOPY CAN TIE BABE RUTH'S HOME-RUN RECORD?

BUT I THOUGHT HANK AARON WAS GOING TO DO THAT...

SNOOPY'S AHEAD OF HIM!

SNOOPY ONLY NEEDS ONE MORE HOME RUN! HE CAN TIE BABE RUTH'S RECORD BEFORE HANK AARON IF THE PRESSURE DOESN'T GET TO HIM...

PRESSURE? WHAT PRESSURE?

SCHOOL STARTS IN TWO WEEKS...

I THOUGHT I HAD ALREADY LEARNED EVERYTHING THERE WAS TO KNOW...

HARDLY

IS IT POSSIBLE FOR ME TO LEARN EVERYTHING THERE IS TO KNOW?

HARDLY

HOW COME I ALWAYS GET CAUGHT IN THE MIDDLE?

YOU KNOW WHAT YOU COULD SAY TO ME IF YOU REALLY LIKED ME?

"I THINK YOU ARE THE NEATEST OF THE NEAT AND THE CUTEST OF THE CUTE!" THAT'S EXACTLY WHAT YOU COULD SAY TO ME IF YOU REALLY LIKED ME...

RATS!

WIN A FEW, LOSE A FEW, CHARLIE BROWN

A NEW PEANUTS BOOK

by Charles M. Schulz

HOLT, RINEHART AND WINSTON

New York • Chicago • San Francisco

Books by Charles M. Schulz

Peanuts
More Peanuts
Good Grief, More Peanuts!
Good Ol' Charlie Brown
Snoopy
You're Out of Your Mind, Charlie Brown!
But We Love You, Charlie Brown
Peanuts Revisited
Go Fly a Kite, Charlie Brown
Peanuts Every Sunday
It's a Dog's Life, Charlie Brown
You Can't Win, Charlie Brown
Snoopy, Come Home
You Can Do It, Charlie Brown
We're Right Behind You, Charlie Brown
As You Like It, Charlie Brown
Sunday's Fun Day, Charlie Brown
You Need Help, Charlie Brown
Snoopy and the Red Baron
The Unsinkable Charlie Brown
You'll Flip, Charlie Brown
You're Something Else, Charlie Brown
Peanuts Treasury
You're You, Charlie Brown
You've Had It, Charlie Brown
Snoopy and His Sopwith Camel
A Boy Named Charlie Brown
You're Out of Sight, Charlie Brown
Peanuts Classics
You've Come a Long Way, Charlie Brown
Snoopy and "It Was a Dark and Stormy Night"
"Ha Ha, Herman," Charlie Brown
The "Snoopy, Come Home" Movie Book
Snoopy's Grand Slam
Thompson Is in Trouble, Charlie Brown
You're the Guest of Honor, Charlie Brown
The Snoopy Festival
Win a Few, Lose a Few, Charlie Brown

Weekly Reader Books presents

WIN A FEW, LOSE A FEW, CHARLIE BROWN

Johathan

from

Ms. Irma